Mandy,

Your last w[...]t

for the cov[...]k!

☺ Mr. Elliot

Idea for a B-Movie

Joe Elliot

Copyright © 2015 Joe Elliot
All rights reserved.
ISBN: 0692536264
ISBN-13: 978-0692536261

FreeScholarPress

For the students of Murrow

Table of Contents

ACKNOWLEDGMENTS

Poems beginning "A few years ago," "Pray, crossed off," and "The dogwood does not think" were first published in *The Magnet*, E.R. Murrow's literary and art magazine.

Poem beginning "Instead of adjusting the speed" first appeared in *BoogLit*.

"For Some Reason" was printed by Anne Noonan as a broadside for a reading given at *The Shed* in Brooklyn, NY.

"Tent as Poem" was included in an on-line gallery of works about/inspired by the Occupy Movement.

Most of these poems found a first audience in and much helpful feedback from "the group": John Faciano, Mickey Erhlich, Rob Elstein, Mauro Bressi, and Daniel Cohen. Thanks!

Joe Elliot

Immediately Following Conception

Joe Elliot

Immediately following conception
everybody spends

the loveliest half hour
of one's life

as a single cell
before one begins

to divide in two
integrities.

for Bob Grenier

The first two years are always silent.
The world goes in
our eyes and ears,
our fingertips and tongues,

and our mute hearts are inundated,
swollen with an accumulating world which,
because it cannot come out,
is still whole,

and so all we can do is shout
or murmur or gurgle or cry,
and that is why our first real words
are always ejaculations,

words like *bird* or *car* or *horse* or *star*,
little pieces of us
flying out of us
with such integral force,

such undivided delight and surprise and release,
out into an outer world
that still exactly corresponds
to a world within

which has already begun to erode
one word at a time.

Making Up Stories

They left the sky in place,
and they left the sun,
and at night the stars and moon
in place in the sky.

And below these they left the mountains and rivers,
the forests and lakes,
the valleys and deserts
and oceans in place.

And left in place also
were the creatures of the air,
and those of the land and water,
as well as every grass and fruit,

every passing cloud,
every glint of light
they left in place,
so that nothing was needed.

And although furthermore they left
every heartbeat and breath,
every desirous impulse
and incidental thought you have,

every intended molecule of you in place
so that nothing was needed,
nevertheless they did leave,
and you do not know what to do,

how to proceed, how to go on
without them, these people
you've thought of
but never met.

This Is How It Happens
from *Summer Hours*

Just when you've put your feet on the floor
    in the morning and you hesitate,
or when you're standing in line at the post office
    and look up,
or when you're moving laundry from the washer
    to the dryer,
or when you're pushing a cart down the produce aisle
    at the store,
or when you're aiming the remote to turn the TV
    off at night,

or when you're stopped at a red light,
hidden behind a windshield and its bent reflections
of cars and fences and yards and houses and
    trees and sky and clouds
and the bright, fracturing glare of the sun,
and your thinking face seizes up,

contorts, and suddenly begins to give forth
dry, wretched little expressions,
ugly, un-cinematic spasms,
weirdly choked, barely audible approximations
of sobs, unwanted and mediocre tears,

tears that do not flow and restore but are
    merely perspired,
squeezed out one by one with reluctance,
each resistant droplet causing you to gag with

an unsatisfying sorrow that is more like vomiting,
more like you've eaten something somewhat bad
    but not really bad,

but nevertheless you find yourself in the grip
    of the dry heaves,
this unprepared for and unfruitful visitation of loss,
this emptying out of emptiness,
this painfully mimed spewing of nothingness,
and then the light turns green,

and you automatically lift your eyes to scan
    the traffic ahead
and check your mirrors for the traffic behind
and your face relaxes back into its habitual setting
and you let your foot off the brake
and begin to move forward.

A Silent Movie

You are dragging your childhood doll around
and no one seems to notice.
When you shuffle down the aisle
looking for a seat on the subway,
the other passengers do not look up
from their newspapers or books,
do not disengage their I-pods
from their ears and open their eyes,
although you'd think the heavy chain
shackling your ankle to the ankle
of the little corpse behind you,
scraping the floor and clanging against
the metal subway pole would provide
sufficient visual and auditory cues.

At the water cooler no one mentions
the terrific odor of her rotting body,
no one remarks on how her doll clothes
are tattered and worn, (providing,
by the way, a nice contrast to the smart
new suit you yourself are wearing),
but nimbly steps over her fetid torso
and exchanges the usual greetings,
a few words about a personal adventure
over the weekend, or a little disaster
with a particular client, or a sudden change
in the weather. And since this smallest
of co-workers always remains a few feet

outside and behind the circle, never chiming in with
an anecdote of her own, never offering
a counter comment or piece of advice,
she is effortlessly overlooked.

At lunch, the *maitre d'* does not ask,
"For two, boss?" as you struggle
to yank your dead little sweetheart
through the door and into the foyer,
her face smooth and worn away,
and with it her mouth and any means
to partake in the sustenance needed
to get out of bed in the morning and
continue this struggle for existence.
No, when you tell him you'll sit at the counter,
he smiles and says, "Very good, boss,"
and leads the way without another word,
without looking back over his shoulder
at what must sound like a small boulder
following your complicated path
through the already packed midday crowd.

Back at work, your supervisor has not offered you
a separate cubicle for this diminutive friend
who follows you to work every day,
has not provided you with a smaller chair
and a smaller desk with smaller drawers,
and a smaller computer and printer,
and a smaller bulletin board,
and a smaller phone and fax machine,

and a set of smaller pens and paper clips,
and smaller sheets of paper,
and a smaller filing cabinet.
Apparently, he must've noticed how dead she is,
how she's always lying on her back,
how her button eyes stare up at the ceiling,
at the cheap, psychosis-inducing fluorescent lighting,
and figures he's never going to get a stitch
of work out of her anyway, and so
doesn't bother to say a word, but leaves you
alone to meet and sometimes exceed
the expectations which have been set for you,
which you do, and perhaps this is why
he feels comfortable looking the other way.

I guess the cloud of flies following the pulpy mess
of what was her body down each aisle
does not deter the other shoppers in any way,
who, with years of expertise, navigate their carts
around your beat-up loved one,
never mentioning the bloody trail,
never mentioning the clumps of hair,
never mentioning how she's always five feet behind
and forgotten. For they are on their own way
to their own kitchens in their own homes
with their own individual plans for dinner,
and do not have time to begin to walk
down the pathway of the uncertain story
of your battered sidekick's life,
an excursion that might prove to be overly

long and complicated, and so they choose,
having quickly glanced down this road
and assessed its bends and bumps, to participate
in denying her existence and say nothing.

At the gym it's no easy feat
for the two of you to get up on the elliptical.
That is why she remains propped
(since she no longer possesses
the vital energy to sit up on her own)
against the unit next to you to wait and watch.
Of course, the perspiring gym member
on this unit next to you does not venture
a comment about this sedentary attitude,
this un-moving way of working out.
For, despite his own perfect abdominal area,
who is he to dictate the right body shape,
the correct exercise routine, the appropriate
quantity of weights and reps for another? No,
this slumped attentiveness may be all
your stuffed little invertebrate can muster,
and so your neighbor respectfully maintains
an effortful straight ahead focus
and refrains from unsolicited advice.

The TV, although it is constantly babbling,
does not offer a caption for the picture
it sees of you two sitting in either corner
of the couch together, your genetic similarities
manifesting now that you've loosened your tie

and let the unguarded weariness of the day
leech out of you and your expression becomes
a little slack-jawed and worn and blurred. You could be
siblings, or an old couple, comfortable enough
to sit without exchanging so much as a glance
or word or even a grunt together for hours.

Nor do the pillows talk,
the pillows who've sworn to give
comfort to whatever head presents itself,
who are discreet enough not to discriminate
between this middle age face,
now smooth and quiet in repose,
and this sewn oval of fabric,
ageless and of indeterminate expression,
although glad in her own blank way, no doubt,
to be done with the day's pulling and tugging,
with the indignity of being slightly behind,
with the insult of no longer being allowed
to exist in any real way,
and to finally be getting some sleep.

Body

Looking at ourselves dissected,
we supply the wonder

that somehow avoided the scalpel,
that somehow was left out

of those particular facts and numbers,
that was not mentioned in the prose

of a catalogue that was edited to impress,
for being overpowered is not wonder,

nor is being struck dumb,
nor is having our eyes sewn shut

in order to maintain a certainty
that claims the upper hand,

which is, at any rate, already
pinned back and flayed,

for we are not what we are looking at,
but what is left over.

Fender Glint

Checking the rear
and side-view mirrors,

engaging the directional
and carefully accelerating

out into traffic,
taking care of these

simple things, waiting
with equanimity to make

that long left hand turn into
the lot behind the pharmacy

to pick up a prescription,
backing into a tight angled spot

in front of the dry cleaners
to drop off a suit and some shirts,

coming to a careful stop
out in the middle of

the Town Hall parking lot to let
the high school softball team

clean your exterior
with their sponges and hoses,

double-parking and putting on
your hazards as you run in

to drop off a few overdue books
at the library by the playground,

and then gliding up
to the edge of the ball field

where your son is waiting for you,
getting out to help him in,

getting to be the parent
behind the wheel

in the front seat,
while your child gets to be

the kid buckled in
in the backseat,

and the two of you
getting to drive and talk or

drive and be
quiet together.

A few years ago
I dressed up
as my dead dad
for Halloween.

I put on a tuxedo
and blew up
a picture of him
in his tuxedo,

and glued his bald head,
his big open mouth,
his crooked teeth,
his jovial expression

and exuberant eyes
to a paper plate
and cut holes in it
and made a mask.

It was disconcerting
how his whole face
was a little too big
and looking to the left,

but what was even scarier
was how I knew
the people we'd meet
trick-or-treating

would have to ask
about my costume,
and I would get to say,
"I'm my dead dad,"

as if it were a piece
of performance art
and my emotional life
were some kind of joke,

something to make
a display of and mine
for its irony,
even though I really did,

and do, miss him,
how he was always
there for me,
withholding and teasing,

talking sideways,
avoiding eye contact,
concocting provocations,
modeling for me

how to make fun
as one walks around
one disaster
after another.

Idea for a B Movie

A boy goes out on a boat with his uncle
into the harbor. A boy goes out on a boat
with his uncle just past the harbor
and learns to fish. A young man goes out
on a boat with his uncle well past the harbor
and they fish all day and bring back a
fine catch. A young man goes out on a boat
all alone well past the harbor out into
the open ocean and fishes all day
and comes back, his boat laden with fish.
A full grown man goes out on a boat
all alone well past the harbor out into
the open ocean and fishes all day
and comes back, his boat laden with fish.
A man in the middle of his life repeats
this sentence every day for weeks
and then months and years. It is a prayer,
and it goes like this: An old man
goes out on a boat all alone well past
the harbor out into the open ocean
beyond the sight of land.

Pray, crossed off
write, crossed off
breakfast
drop-off, crossed off

on-line course work
bike (fix flat), crossed off
fill out on-line application
follow-up e-mails

swim, crossed off
read pp. 86-88
call Ted, crossed off
call Barbara, crossed off

go to Key Food, crossed off
bike ride with Walter, crossed off
meditate
don't think

dinner and dishes, crossed off
sweep and pick up, crossed off
weed garden
cross it all off

put it all up on the cross
and drive a nail through
each hand and foot
and from that dreadful robotic height

review your day
forgive yourself
forgive others
get some sleep, crossed off

Calypso at the Airport

Another
darker

more apocalyptic
I can't quite remember

dream. The eucalyptus
sways. The cryptic

need stays, this bright
sudden nullity

left over,
under

a slightly different tree,
its unstated need

for eye contact
averted. O,

this strange
unreadable shard

that's me
remaindered.

The Window Sill

I dreamt that I woke up
and my glasses were next to me on the bed
and I hadn't rolled over on them
and I handed them to my Dad

who was standing next to the bed
silent and a little fuzzy
in the darkness of the room
and I was glad

and went back to sleep
and when I woke up
my glasses really were there
and I hadn't rolled over on them

and I remembered my dream
and the room beyond
the rumpled bedding was pale
and clear and still

and I picked up the glasses
and placed them on the window sill

Joe Elliot

The Stewardesses

Joe Elliot

The stewardesses are getting older and older.
Soon we will have to attend to them.

They will be strapped into ambulatory devices
rolling down the aisle

handing out all manner of medication
on an altogether different kind of flight

high above the clouds.

Climbing All Over Each Other

My horsing around with you
expresses a joy that implies

a connection to an identical
but infinite horsing around joy

that I need. Everything is good.
Everything is all right.

Why don't you climb up
on my back, He said,

and I'll make silly celestial
twinkling sounds, the sounds

of stars, the sounds implied by
the mere idea of those tiny,

tiny animals down there
climbing all over each other.

Non-personal

I don't say hello.
I don't want to muck up our relationship with talk.
I simply walk to the same part of the same park
and sit down on the same bench
and wait.

When I start to think about what I may have to do
later that day, or what I should or shouldn't have said
the day before, or how I've messed up my marriage,
botched my career, how I'll be found out, exposed,
and end up unloved and unable to love,

I try to return my awareness to the bench,
how it feels to be sitting there,
how its wood feels against my legs and back,
how still it is and unmoving,
and how well it supports my body and breath,

and sometimes wonder if it's breathing too,
if it can feel my body the way I can feel its body,
if it knows how much I look forward to these
twenty minutes each day, but I do not say a word.
I don't want to mess up the moment with words.

That House

Waiting for the honest thing to write,
that to which you have a secret
connection, something that might be opened,

something that is wrapped up in the everyday,
so that it is overlooked,
left on the doorstep of the house.

It is cold out, and very early in the morning.
Wisps of fog from the gray sea
approach and circle the container.

Intimacy

I always leave the front door unlocked
and the kitchen light on. I make sure
the Mr. Coffee's set up, and put a plate
of oatmeal cookies out on the counter,
and leave a note: "Help yourself. There's
cream in the fridge and a sugar bowl
next to the stove. Anne's mom's silver
is on the top shelf above the sink.
We hardly use it. The home computer
is sleeping in the office off the hall upstairs,
and our password, a scramble of names
and birthdays, is scribbled on a post-it
affixed to the window sill. My laptop's charging
on the kitchen table. The flat screen TV,
of course, is hanging in the living room,
the dark open area you just walked through
to get to the kitchen. My wallet and anything
I found in my pockets today is in a tray
on top of my bureau in the bedroom
at the top of the stairs. Anne's jewelry box
is on hers. If it makes you feel more comfortable
you can go back outside and use the ladder
I left leaning against the eaves in the back.
From there, you can get in the open window
quite easily, but before you enter may I suggest
you pause and turn and have a look
at the night sky floating above the willow's

silhouette. Tonight should be a full moon, too!
Or perhaps you'd prefer the alleyway
where a crowbar rests against a half window
to the basement. It is quiet there,
and dark, and you can work in peace,
and the sound of clattering glass
in the middle of the night is a pleasure
difficult to frown on. I do not hide cash
or valuables under mattresses or bury them
in the back of closets, although you're welcome
to turn them over or dig through them
to your heart's content. My passport
is in the top drawer of my desk. The car keys
are hanging on a hook by the front door.
If you are confused by the location of anything,
or if you feel the need to ask any questions,
or, above all, if you find yourself at any time feeling
uncomfortable or scared or ashamed or bad
in any way, please feel free to nudge me gently
on the arm and wake me up to talk about it.
You don't want to carry that stuff around."

Sleeping Soundly

Three joint compound buckets on our bed
under the strategic places I poked holes
to keep the rainwater from building up
and soaking through and sagging the whole
ceiling sodden suddenly collapsing on
our bed of vows. Instead, Anne

out cold and then hot and cold again
in a mass of bedding twisting between buckets,
and me on my back on the throw rug
in the alley between bed and wall,
my head almost out the door,
listening to the music of the three buckets,

their three distinct levels of water,
their shapely plinks and plunks,
thinking how to stay married you need
a hammer and a hole punch,
and the ability to sleep through
anything and anywhere.

Some houses
do not have
a cellar.

In that case,
it could be
a garage,

or an attic,
or even a closet,
wherever

you store
that stuff
you might need

later.
You must
go there

with the lights out.
You must
feel your way

along the wall
and sit
down in

the middle of
all of it
and wait.

Talking back
as a way

of coming back
to life.

Talking back you need
the prior version

to talk
back to.

You need the leg
of an animal

for your own leg
to become animate.

You need the compressed
sedimentary accumulation

of millions and millions of
years of tiny souls

to put a tiger
in your tank,

to depress your pedal,
engage your gears,

and drive to C-Town
to buy that leg.

Recitation

I'm with Dexter.
We are in a cavernous room
walking on a rim that spirals,
like the inside groove of a nut or lid,
upwards, making our way to the safety door
at the far end. When we get there
Dexter is right behind me,
and waiting for us on the other side
of the steel door is what appears to be a woman
wearing glasses, only her eyes are too big
and don't blink. They dominate the small
thick paned security window through which
she seems to be watching us. There is a sense
that this woman is really a creature,
that the woman is only the form
the creature has taken. There is a sense
that if it wanted to it could easily
break through the gray door to get to us,
but it is waiting for me to choose
to open it. I'm unsure what to do. It moves
its face and shows its teeth,
which aren't quite right or human,
in what I realize is meant to be a smile,
an expression of mirth or laughter,
but because its face is bloated
and does not really wear an expression,
any at all, let alone one of warmth

or mirth or laughter, I come to see
that this thing's face is really a mask,
that I cannot tell its identity
or intentions in relation to me. What is it
waiting for anyway? What does it
want from me? Why does it
seem to need me? Is it really
a part of me? I tell Dexter
to prepare himself. We are going
home. Our plan is to say
the Lord's Prayer loudly
and then open the door.

Two Men

The long ears of the Buddha
represent the kingdom he owned,
the pendants and gems
that hung from those princely lobes
and weighed them down
and stretched them
to the point where he had to renounce such things
in favor of a fantastic nothingness
he was able to overhear
as a stranger wandering roads
in outer provinces he'd once ruled.

The long nails of Howard Hughes
represent the empire he founded and grew
and which continued to grow
long after he had died
to it. The publicity stunts, the startling
deal-making, the starlets,
the constant need to be seen,
although he withdrew from all these playthings
and fashioned an enormous bird of spruce
as his final disappearing act,
his innocence did not save him,
for all these empty playthings,
refusing to be withdrawn from, stuck,
and his nails had nowhere to turn,
and so they grew
and grew.

Joe Elliot

A Good Perch

The birds did not alight on his shoulder
because of the halo. They did not see
a universal sign of saintliness
and therefore hasten to this beacon

of exemplary peace and simplicity,
as humanly attractive
as these qualities may be,
and then lovingly coo in his ear.

It is more likely that he was so inward and still,
so lost in the present,
just standing there in the rain
and sun for hours and hours,

that they mistook him for
the branch of a tree,
or the top of a wall or fence or rock,
and so landed on his sturdy shoulder

simply because it afforded them a good perch
and purchase, for which, to his credit,
as he did not understand it or anything as transaction,
Francis did not make them pay.

Thus, the halo, in honor of his utter lack of humanity,
his wholesale inability to respond,
his unwillingness to simply swat or shoo
or even flinch or mutter a word,

was conferred on him by the birds themselves
when they flew about his head in a whirr
to show the faint glow of the inanimate
they can everywhere see but we cannot.

Love

Just before the collision
the two celestial bodies,

as they near each other,
more and more veer

out of their approximate
but separate orbits

directly at each other,
obeying the law of attraction,

seeking the center
of the other,

giving in at the very
last moment to commitment,

abandoning any and all
notions of accident.

Lullaby

Husband and wife.
Late at night.
The wife is talking.
The husband

wants her to hush.
She won't.
He puts a pillow
over his head.

She leans over
and pushing it down
whispers in
the pillow's ear.

INVESTIGATION

Joe Elliot

Rah Rah

Even though
there really isn't
an other,

and therefore
there isn't
even a you,

try to
be whole
heartedly for

your side,
and act as if
there were

such a thing,
assigned to
such a you.

Joe Elliot

A movie in which
the characters are very small,
and we don't know which
ones to identify with,

and we sit there,
isolated in the dark,
unable to participate in
the dream of plot,

and still the tiny images
up on the screen
continue to flicker
in a workmanlike way.

The Holidays

Even that servant,
the one of indeterminate age,
the one that arrived
first at the feast
to set up tables and chairs
and lay out silverware and glasses
and arrange flowers and light candles
and attend to iced tabs of butter,

the one that then brought out
with aplomb astounding platters of food
and re-filled glasses
and fielded special request
after special request
and quietly cleaned up
that drunken mess
in the men's room,

even that one, after the last
dish has been dried and put away,
after all the hidden debris
of such a holiday celebration
has been swept up and mopped
and bagged and brought to the curb,
after everyone else has
long since gone home,

even this one, the one
that no one notices,
must retire to his room
at the top of the stairs
and take off his suit
and hang it up
and climb into bed
and turn off the light.

The empty
winter woods.

Birds still.
Able to see

for lack of leaves.
The louder

more musical
stream thrums

over icicled
roots and rocks.

The world
as cavity.

The chest
as drum.

At the bottom of the stairs he saw
a shadow moving without its body.
It was killing time there on the landing,
a vague blob of freedom and dimness
blending into the space where the stair
met the wall. Maybe it was nothing

when a crow perched on the streetlamp,
when a baby down the block cried out
in its crib, when the voracious refrigerator
spilled its light into the dark kitchen,
or when, for lack of a better word, students
were roaming the hallways looking for

connection, some clue as to who
they might be. Maybe it was a mistake
to put faith in what he saw, to give shape
to what was shapeless, to cast light
on what was black, to ask a question
of one who offered answers.

The dog
following the woman
from room
to room.

The steady
tail movement.
How the furniture
looms

and marks
the way.
The door,
and then outside.

The watery
brown eyes.
The lack
of any need

for words
made manifest.
The weird light
and its dust.

The obedient
garden itself
also
a halo.

Above the trees
a hawk disappears
into the white
morning fog.

On the sidewalk
below, a man,
bundled up
against the damp,

is thinking his thoughts
to himself
as he walks
his dog.

The two of them,
connected loosely
by a leash,
move along nicely.

The more
you think
you lack

The more lack
you think
you have

In silence comes the frost,
the movement of the first
pebble of the avalanche,
the sudden urge to lean on your horn
in what it turns out you thought
to be bad traffic.

In darkness prepares the present,
the re-emphasis of a recent
event you did not notice
at all in the first place,
and now here it is in your heart,
its sullen mouth shut.

Without any sensation arrives the guidance
to the innermost cell
of the vee's lead goose,
itself all outward and loud
fanfare for itself and home,
wherever that is.

Our days are numbered.
On the upper right hand corner
of each of them is a tag.
This one reads: 18,549,
quite a lovely,
if alarmingly
long, number, below which

in 10 point Courier
is specified further:
"A cool and crisp day.
A day of joy.
On this day
you may
receive a visitor."

I slip this day
into the front of the file
and shove the file
back into the drawer.
I have my orders.
I am ready
for any visitor.

Go Fish

When the captain
blows the horn

the fishermen
pull in their lines,

put up their rods,
and go into the cabin

to resume their game
of five card stud.

And the party boat
begins to move,

nosing about the open
ocean, the same

glittering surface, the same
unyielding face for miles

in every direction,
sending blind waves

into the dark
to flush out fish.

Person

Still waiting to see
how you'll turn out
when you've already
turned out.

You don't have to
worry about that
anymore.
I'll tell you.

You've turned out to be
a person
waiting to see
how he's turned out.

Joe Elliot

Achilles

In island cultures,
where space is at a premium
and everyone knows
everyone else,

they dig three or four
times as deep,
straight down
into the rock,

and stack the coffins
one on top
of the other,
and bury them that way,

along with the allure
of occupying a higher
or lower
station in life.

Investigation

Who killed him?
Interview all suspects.
All are human.
Every one of them

has an alibi. No one
killed him. His parents
and siblings,
his friends and co-workers,

his wife and kids,
every teacher and priest
he ever had,
all of them

killed him.
It was a mob,
a slow-moving
irresistibly smiling

mob of daily
human interaction,
love laced with fear
and doubt,

and look
how willing
even happy he was
to go.

Denouement
for John Faciano

It's weird
how in English
we tie up
loose ends,

while in French
we unravel
the knot
of the plot,

but in Greek
we are always
three,
two to

spin and span and
one to cut

Idea for a B-movie

Joe Elliot

I try to get a run in
before the storm hits.
I make it halfway
around the park

before I strain my calf
and have to pull up
and hobble back
the long way around the lake.

Not knowing when I'll get out again,
I decide to pick up
a half gallon of milk
at the corner deli.

Inside, there's been a run
on batteries and bottled water,
and the conversation in the aisles
and over the counter

keeps turning on the eye,
where it is on the radar,
when it's supposed to hit land,
whom it's going to hover over and harm.

Outside, the sky is low.
My modest provision
is under my arm.
By the back alley

of the apartment building
the neighborhood calls The Castle,
a low, solitary bush
is fat with sparrows

hidden to the eye
but not the ear.
They know something and are
all talking at once.

Winter Scene

Two fat squirrels
camping out
at the feeder
on the table.

One's taking his time
having his fill
of what'd been
given to all.

The other's on the rim
facing out
warding off
the bigger birds:

cardinals and jays
who swoop and squawk,
or hop about
the thin snow,

making an occasional
sortie from
behind the plastic
leg of a chair.

The smaller ones,
sparrows and wrens,
on the porch's perimeter
pretend to be

too busy to pay
much attention. Yet,
when the door opens
all of them,

afraid of the hand
that holds the seed,
flee
to neighboring trees

where they cluster and chitter
their various songs
about who gets what
and why.

Why Busses On Longer Routes Love Each Other And Tend To Clump

The bus that already has more passengers
begins to slow down because it needs to make
more stops to let this greater number of passengers
off, but, because it's slowing down and beginning
to run a little bit behind schedule, the passengers
waiting for this bus to arrive at last begin
to accumulate more and more at each stop,
so that this same slow bus begins to slow down
even more, every stop it stops at five or ten or even
fifteen passengers waiting to squeeze on or off,
so that it takes this bus longer and longer to load
and unload, the aisles beginning to crowd
with passive aggression, the passenger attitudes
beginning to erode, the spirit of mutual respect
and cooperation more and more beginning to ebb,
as this embarking and disembarking of passengers
becomes a longer and longer trial, more filled
with muttered interjections and askance glances,
with the close odor of damp clothes,
with crying children held by wrists, meanwhile,
the busses behind this bus that has begun
to slow down have begun to speed up
more and more, to run a little bit ahead of schedule,
since that same bus slowing down ahead of them
has begun to pick up a greater number of passengers
from each stop at which they'd begun to accumulate,

certain passengers lining up on the long line
to get on who wouldn't have made this bus at all
if it had still been on schedule, but would've
had to wait for the busses behind this one
to pick them up, so that there's fewer and fewer
passengers for the busses following the slower
one ahead to be picked up, so that their loading
and unloading takes less and less time, so that the
second and third busses begin to catch up to this
first one that has slowed down so much more
and is now way behind schedule, so that the
distances between the one ahead and the ones
behind have begun to decrease, and all of the busses
may even be able to see each other from a distance,
just a few blocks away, looming in the rear
or side view mirrors, the slower one in front now
stopping for quite a while at every stop on every block,
while the ones behind may already have begun
to skip over a stop or two, since the passengers
waiting at a stop may already have been picked up
by the bus in the lead, which, at this point, can hardly
be said to be moving at all, and, since there's less
and less distance between the busses, there's less
and less opportunity for new passengers to accumulate
at each stop between the three busses, although
the ones ahead of the three now throng, an unhappy
thickness of passengers glancing at watches, checking
phones, craning necks, squinting down the avenue
to see if the appointed bus, or any bus at all, is

on its way, or, likewise, there may not be enough
passengers on the busses behind waiting to get off
to warrant a stop, there may not be a certain
passenger waiting to get off at a certain stop,
so that that certain stop is skipped, eliminating
that time that might've been spent disembarking
and embarking, so that the busses behind draw closer
and closer, less and less behind, so that pretty soon
the three are only a stop or two away from each other,
are traveling in clumps, the first one overloaded
standing room only, the second one having a few seats
open only two or three passengers standing here
and there in the aisle, and the third one nearly empty,
careening after the first two, trying to catch up.

Off to Work

The early morning
rain has stopped,

and a car has left
a perfectly dry

shadow of itself
behind in the now

open parking spot.

The Hero's Dream

Instead of waking up
and brushing your teeth
and eating breakfast
and going to work
and working
and then coming home
and eating dinner
and watching TV
and going to bed

Instead of that
waking up knowing you're on some kind of quest
and brushing your teeth
and eating breakfast
and going to work
and working
and then coming home
and eating dinner
and watching TV
and going to bed
and dreaming
the hero's dream

My parents were at the hospital.
They were standing
in their street clothes,
on either side of the bed,

which was empty.
They were are not looking at the bed,
which was unwrinkled and smooth,
but at each other.

I could hear them talking about
how I was going to be re-born,
how they therefore had to re-name me
and were thinking about *Daniel*,

which I've always felt was a weird name.
I wanted to say something,
but the bed was newly made
and the sheets were tight,

pressing down on my mouth and face,
which weren't even there yet,
so I couldn't wriggle free
or say a word.

The Unmoving

The unmoving white
and black pony moment

mounted to a steel
rod going down into

a machine on the sidewalk
in front of the grated

pharmacy on Coney Island
Avenue disappeared

when the double doors
closed and the bus

pulled away that early
November morning.

Joe Elliot

This morning the bus smells
like fresh upholstery,
like stainless steel and little fingers
holding on tight,

like a can of tennis balls
when it's first cracked open
and it sends forth its faint
whiff of fuzz,

like something moth-balled
in the back of a closet
in an apartment complex
somewhere between Ditmas and Midwood,

like a tinted window
or a reverse photo of the sky,
the sun all black, the storm clouds
weirdly iridescent,

like that invisible importance
a flock of pigeons can see and circle
high above a rooftop,
but we cannot,

like an eleven year old miniature man,
his hair smartly parted
by his mother for what everyone
always tells him is his job,

school, like inert flesh
relaxed into a winter jacket,
bones held by a plastic seat,
rocked and swayed by predictable motion,

like that dark residue of repetition
at the back of your oven
you stick your head into
and try to scrape with a spatula

or spoon. I guess it must've been
the detergent they use.

Today

I thought of
giving myself
the gift of
not worrying about

what people think,
even what
I think,
just doing what

presents itself
to do,
maybe even enjoying
the little

bits of it,
what
I couldn't have thought
to think of.

The dogwood does not think
he's on a crappy side street
somewhere in Midwood. He does not suspect
the hubcap and the broken bottle
at his feet might not be there.

They're there, as is the cool April air,
and the dented pick-up truck,
and the crumbling curb cut.
Yes, the hydrant halfway down the block,
the candy wrapper that catches

what's left of that hedge
bordering the lot on the corner
are all he knows. He does not say, "No,
I will not crown this mediocre afternoon,
with my delicate bloom."

Indeed, he seems as surprised
by these unearthly apparitions,
these white white blossoms,
as is the condom by the drainpipe squashed,
as is the empty coffee can

down the middle of the street kicked
by a kid, head down, as if he owns
nothing, nothing is his, and he,
too, is only participating
in this thing called Spring.

People have begun to give themselves over
to irrational numbers. They have stopped eating

their bowls of toasted oats at the kitchen counter.
They have stopped waving to their neighbors

on the corner. Instead of walking out the front door
in the morning, they have dropped anchor

in the hallway or in the bathroom or wherever
they were when the fervor first took hold of them.

Yes, they are lying there with pencil and paper.
They have committed themselves to being in the pure

moment of calculation, to standing by their number
steadfastly as it mutates through its progression

of pre-ordained surprises. Does it really
go on forever? There they are, on the shoulder

of the highway, happily undertaking this long longer
longest division on family-size rolls of paper.

They find this figuring it out better by far
than licking the backs of so many stamps per hour,

than lining up at dusk to be stuffed one by one
into the mouth of mass transit. They find comfort

in the generosity of numbers. They wonder
how something so simple, so compact and small,

can generate gift after gift? They're still on task,
sitting at a picnic table in a Dairy Queen parking lot,

partially obscured by the rising towers of paper,
on top of each of which they've placed an alarm

clock or a flower pot or an old boot to keep their
labors from blowing away. They find this new way

of life preferable to flying halfway around the world
to shoot a civilian, to pushing a metal cart

down a canned goods aisle, to putting a dollar bill
in one slot to get a bag of chips out of another,

to calling a lovely old doorway an egress,
to lining the perimeter of schoolyards everywhere

with sandbags and razor-wire. They hate calculators.
They prefer to do the arithmetic and show all their work.

Joe Elliot

That is why
we are always
fascinated by
what is happening
between buildings,

why the deep shade
of some alleyway
is where a squirrel is glimpsed
scrambling headfirst
down a drainpipe,

and why we gaze
out the long windows of trains
into the backs of yards
at abandoned vehicles
and derelict sheds,

and why we can't quite grasp
or let go of
a few green weeds
growing out of a crack
in the gutter,

and how one's own life
by overweening implication might also
be only a glimpse
by someone else
of something other.

Divination

There are two cliffs
with waterfalls,
and they are facing each other,
only it's not water it's milk
flowing from
these two precipices.

And it's like this:
you feel like you have to choose
one of them,
but they're identical,
and identically facing you
for a reason.

Therefore,
if you can stand it,
you are to refrain
from choice,
from any solution whatsoever,
and just sit there

between the two
and trust this flow of milk
from the lips of rock that jut
out from either
side of you
for a reason.

Joe Elliot

Idea for a B-movie

A week ago, I open the fridge.
When I reach in to grab the milk
I notice a puddle on the shelf.
I check the bottom of the carton.
It's moist, but it's difficult
to see where it's seeping from.
So I pour a little into my coffee,
wipe down the shelf, and put
the carton on a saucer and back
into the fridge. Problem solved.

Three days ago, I carry a bag
of groceries into the kitchen
and set it down on the counter.
When I take hold of the milk
to put it away, it gives a little,
and when I swing it across
the kitchen to the open refrigerator,
the carton caves in and wriggling
out of my grasp falls to the floor.
At my feet, a pure white puddle
begins to spread over the linoleum,
silently nosing its way under
the stove. I run to get a towel.

Idea for a B Movie

Yesterday, I'm walking back
from the store. I'm behind Karl.
I notice the bottom of his backpack
is dark and damp. Its back corner
is dripping onto his socks and calf.
He stops and starts to pull things out.
The Wayfarers by Knut Hamsun
is a pulpy mess. His Yankees cap
hangs sodden and shapeless. The screen
of his digital camera is now a milky
non-functional white. The carton itself,
which appears to have unfolded
and flattened itself out in the pack,
Karl now hurls to the sidewalk
and mushes beneath his shoes.

At this very moment, all over the world
cartons are coming undone
and cool milk is escaping,
pooling, gathering strength and spreading,
running through open doors,
seeping into and whitening
whatever gets in its way.

Off the Board, Out the Window

If those two parallel lines
that are traveling forever

out past the illusion of the blue
bowl of the sky

into space, out past anything
that might offer even a little

resistance, past particles and air,
past heat and distance and any

meaningful sense of self and other,
toward some tiny twinkling

they see but which has ceased,
along with time, to exist,

were to bend and meet
and break themselves up,

and these resulting individual
segments were to curl

and knot themselves
into curious shapes,

and these curious shapes
were to arrange themselves

into words and lines,
they might look like this.

Prospect Park Southwest and Seeley Street

A painting is different.
A painting has trees
and a sky
and a lake
and a shore that rims the lake.

It has one or two
street signs as well,
and a mother
and a stroller
in the early morning.

But in this painting the tips
of the branches
do not sway,
and dawn's pinking clouds
are not even a little bit

on the move. Nor does this
painting include
you as a part
of its landscape,
a very small part,

but one that inhales
and exhales
a bigger picture.
And this painting
cannot feel

the way
your cheek
can feel
the breath
of winter.

Joe Elliot

Early March

After a day
of hallways
and classrooms,

of industrial
tiling and intercom
announcements,

of constant and close
fluorescent
interactions,

the beautiful
cold blue
evening sky,

the strange
illumination
of clouds,

the faceless distances,
and the slight
epiphany of green

and debris
wherever the silver
snow has receded

wake me
on my way
to the car.

SCRAMBLED EGGS

Joe Elliot

Idea for a B Movie

Last night a man
put on a mask
that was made
of scrambled eggs.

Slowly the egg
spread over the holes
where the recessed eyes
and mouth would be.

All rubbery and yellow
the mask began to
chew and sink
into itself.

Joe Elliot

Communion

That he might be
immanent

makes the world
his body,

opens your eyes
to what you see,

opens your ears
to what you hear,

makes you reconsider
the air you breathe,

what you reach
out for and touch,

taste
and eat.

Governor's Island Art Fair
for Maureen Nolette

I liked looking through the partly open door
into that attic, with its odorous peeling paint,
empty except for a wide screen on which
a bay's slowly undulating gray waters
and the extremely gradual emergence of
what must've been parts of a headland
and bridge through the wispily shifting fog
were being projected, as if these eventually
implied pieces of a landscape were partial
secrets within secrets, wrapped in their slow
silence and motion, and the way to release
these secrets was to ride wave after wave of
trying not to do much but watch and wait.

I also enjoyed the room dominated by life-size
cut-out paper furniture hanging from the ceiling
by string, so that you were invited to experience
this space by having to choose a path to walk
through it or find a place within its brightly
painted confusion to stand, or by brushing up
against its floating clutter, as if you were
in a dream or an old story book, or some three
dimensional child's demonstration of Cubism.

I felt admiration, too, for the dogmatism of four
small paintings whose surfaces were fabricated
out of glue and shredded documents, a mostly
black and white, with occasional splashes of red
or blue, mixture that was evenly applied to
the canvasses' fronts and sides, resulting in a
mysterious texture out of which truncated words
and half phrases emerged like oraclular
blades of grass or Astroturf, a kind of crazy,
post-logo-centric armor (what were those
incantations that we chanted so long ago, and
what were the obscure reasons we were chanting
them?), with straight ahead, pretentious titles,
like *Historiography #3* or *Historiography #4*.

Of course, the room filled with floor to ceiling
scroll drawings and watercolors that rolled out to
your feet was stunning. I liked the devotion to
difficulty that was implied by the fantastic, swirling
intricacy of lines, as if the images stood for and
were the product of a profound life practice, a
beautiful discipline that might make us better,
might occupy us and focus us so we that might
stop making such foolish and disastrous choices.

I was floored, as well, by the two clean walls
that met and were joined by continuous and regularly
wavy rows of white ribbon mounted perpendicularly
to the also white surface on standard, nearly
invisible pins, so that the installation itself
was a miracle of fragility and precision and restraint

Idea for a B Movie

(look, ma! mere ribbon and pencil and pins!),
so that, while the material stood out, it actually
disappeared too, as it was only the sturdy shadow
of the white on white we were seeing, not its
being or essence, but its domestic function, how
it took up and displaced space. But, perhaps

my favorite piece from the show came later,
after all the tramping up and down stairwells
was over, and I had found a moment to sit down
in a smaller room, and looking up at the parallel
slats through which the late afternoon light
and all the festive and floating faraway sounds
of the fair came, I glimpsed an intricate web,
glinting where it intersected the mote-filled bands
as it extended from a corner above the door
diagonally back and down, a kind of makeshift
woven shanty roof, high up and over the bowl
where I was squatting. I squinted; almost lost
in the middle of this elaborate act of faith flung
over the void was this response: two pairs of
tiny green eyes, horseflies held fast, twitching,
and as I reached for the paper to finish the job
at hand I considered how authentically this work
had been installed, how efficient and self-effacing
was its design, how it'd even been given
to the viewer to interact with it and maximize
its function, and how I might choose to
help reimburse further this humble artist
for her labor by refraining to flush.

The Sign

Squiggly
lines

floating up
from a cup.

Black
block lettering

forever
aflame.

Wake up
and smell

the emblem
of your

being there
in your dream

chair
making your way

down
the page.

Debtor's Blame

I know
I owe
you a lot
but I cannot

pay you back
when you keep
sending me back
to prison

Circa

Like a rowboat about to bump into the prow
of an ocean-liner and its solitary mariner
bare-chested stands up and shaking his fist shouts,
at the exact moment this approaching mountain
of inertia sends forth its stultifying whistle, words
which this poem was unable to record.

However, the movie version does cut to the girl
with a powder blue bow in her hair. She is leaning
precariously over the rail, tugging at her mother's
Magyar sleeve, jabbing at the character
building air with her finger, "Look!
There's a little man down there! A little man

in a little boat!" Scanning the waves with her silver
lorgnettes, the mother does see something,
something shadowy and is it upside down?
like Peter on the far wall of her *camera obscura*
to a brief and polite applause,
emerge and then disappear into a trough.

Idea for a B Movie

I am already nostalgic
for this moment.

I am already seeing it
as having happened
here, forever, the cat

curled up on a stack
of papers to be graded
on the table, the afternoon

sun preserving
this instance of repose.

I am already hearing
the low hum of the pump
in the other room,

the gentle burbling
of water into the tank,

and from here already
and easily I am imagining
the fish themselves,

alert and patterned and circling
the bright plastic
coral rooted in blue
and pink pebbles,

and all these objects:
the darting fish
and the tank,

the standing lamp
and the old sofa,

the back pack by the back door,
the pile of books
that mustn't be disturbed,

derive their weighty
meaning from being gone.

A Romantic Poem

For so long it had to be mounds of phlox
alternating neatly with mounds of day lilies;
or the shapely fronds of ferns and hostas
in the deep shade of a side lawn by a pond;

or a wall of pink tea roses lining a bed
of herbs: rosemary and sage and lavender; or rows
of lilacs, how they had to mature and meet
above forming a walkway of fragrance.

It is only now that you are leaving that you notice
the violets pushing up from the gap in the steps
leading up to the Post Office; or the rogue
cherry tomato plant clinging to the shallow

pool of dirt by the downspout behind your neighbor's
garbage bins; or the morning glories festooning
the chain link fence that separates your block
from the empty lot at the end of the street;

or the Queen Anne's lace blooming at the feet
of a guard rail by the highway embankment;
or the young ailanthus shooting up at the back
of an alley, trying to find the sky.

In The Distance A Tiny Bird Breathes Fire Into a Cloud For No Apparent Reason

The surplus of what we see is not an affront.
The dragon on the outer edge of the map
is not there to disrespect us, to make us feel
small and unloved. Its scales are green and shine
to the exact degree that our imaginations shine.
The enormous *ficus* is not putting us down
when its multiple trunks rise and twist the sky,
is not threatening us when it drops its young limbs
down to colonize all the dirt and darkness it can,
or when it snakes its roots out laterally, making waves
of the perfectly shaped shade under its canopy.

We do not take a pick ax and split open a rock
just because the rock is sitting there in the sun,
and is silent, and seems only for itself. No,
it is not an insult that the person on the other side
of the bed is a self-contained entity, a mystery
with its own set of strange rules and agendas
that have nothing to do with us. Thus, we do not
drill into this sleepy substance and dynamite it
to make way for our road; nor do we take it
personally should a stray shoot seem to want to
entwine a neck or two on its way to the ground.

No, we sidestep these wayward impulses and say
thank you for all the foot and hand holds its surplus
of sealed-off activity has inadvertently afforded us,
and climb up to the topmost branches where we sway
from the wind and the view of all that's not us.

Archeology

It's hard to pin down exactly how many years
ago it became her habit to sleep on the day bed
in the library. It is only my dreamy expedition
down the hallway in the middle of the night,
when I fumble the switch and the bathroom looms
into reality and some of the light spilling out
angles across this temporary encampment,
that I get a glimpse into the incomprehensible
gravity of all that time having fled and left her here,
on top of some sheets, curled up on her side,
an arrangement of limbs, which are way too thin
but knobby where they join. Her waxy skin hangs
limply from her frame, and her damp white hair,
clinging to her sunken and wrinkled but peaceful face,
still child-like and trusting in sleep, slightly stirs
when the fan moves back and forth across this scene
in the heat, while the rest of her does not.

I am sleeping
on a mattress that goes
down and down
like a well.

I am riding a horse to death,
only the horse is on its side,
and it's still warm,
and I can feel its heart.

We are in a hurry to get there,
and its hairs keep rising
to the surface of the mattress,
coming through the bed pad and sheet,

to prick me awake
within this dream of a life
that keeps on writing and writing itself
no matter what I do.

I pull on a rope
and out of the gloom
a bucket of cool words comes up.
A little spittle is forming

on the corner of its mouth
where the bit we no longer need
used to lodge.
We are done with lodging.

Joe Elliot

We are traveling at high speed,
and are almost there.
I stroke its head
and brush its damp hair.

It's only a matter
of lying down now
for a little nap, for just a few
moments of rest.

Idea for a B Movie

In the dream, the dream knows
every detail of the dream.
The other person in the dream
has a face and a name
that the dream always easily recognizes,
although I do not.

We are sitting in a place
that is not far from a lake,
I think, in a small town.
It feels like my first time there,
and while everything,—the nondescript
tables, the egg-shaped cobblestones,
the weird ladder leaning against the weird tower,
the cobwebs (or is it moss?) in my hair,—
with a vivid clarity loom
before me, the dream, having lived in this
mysterious backwater all its life,
accepts these marvels the way you might accept
a package wrapped in brown paper
from the mailman you knew as a kid.
He is wearing a pith helmet and it is
a very hot day.

When the waiter comes to take our order,
he seems in a hurry. He points to the other tables.
At one, an elderly couple is working its way
through wide dessert saucers. At another,
a filthy boy sips a tall lemonade
while his faithful terrier watches

from the opposite seat. In the corner,
a lady from another, lonelier, era
stares out a window, which is, or course,
somehow an outside window.

He tries to explain to us how he has to play
the waiter in all these other dreams,
even the empty dreams of the unoccupied tables,
and somewhat aggressively right away
starts writing something down in his pad,
something that makes him chuckle to himself,
although I do not remember
having actually told him, or myself,
for that matter, what it is exactly
that I want.

When he finally goes, I turn my head
and there is a new person, a stranger
who is vaguely hostile sitting in the seat
of what must've been my lover,
and we are no longer at a table
in a café in the plaza of a provincial town,
but on a train speeding through the mountains
at night. I am surprised, and not a little
anxious about tunnels, and have a free-floating
sense of loss that the dream decides
is shallow. The dream is never at a loss,
or surprised or anxious or afraid. The dream
always knows how to dream and what it is
it is dreaming.

A Single Raindrop Falls On An Open Black Umbrella

Every night you fall through the doors of sleep.
This obedience to gravity is experienced as
weightlessness, and soon you are flying.
In the mornings, when you open an eyelid
and notice your body and limbs are still inert
and heavy, still just on the other side of
these doors, you wonder if you will ever
be able to move them again, if they will respond
to your will, if this breath you are breathing
is something this body you are looking at
is still participating in. It is then that you sit up
and the world's weight returns to you,
and pausing on the bed's edge you consider the day,
which seems to be yours again, and manage
to get up and walk down the hall.

One night, when you fall through these doors
and sink into your mattress which is now a cloud,
or a rowboat on a mountain lake,
or the benign palm of an open hand,
or the feathered back of a winged creature,
you notice there is something different
about this dream. In the dream, you understand
every detail of the dream. You see them
for what they are: pieces of a lonely world

that wants to return. But you don't care. You keep
falling, and when you look at your feet
and try to move your toes, you can't.
Nor can you move your legs and arms.
Nor can you move your mouth
to greet the sun or even the people
who come through the doors
and then hurry back out.

Yesterday, On My Way Back From Maximart

I saw a black cat
on the bicycle path.
She was shy,
but not too shy.

As I approached,
she withdrew from the path
and into the hedge,
and obscured by the thicket

of branches and leaves,
looked out at me.
I did not make a move
to get any closer,

but said some pleasant things,
and she did not run.
We stood our ground
each of us eyeing the other,

me with my brown eyes,
and her with her yellow
ones flashing from
the leafy shadows,

until the bag of groceries
grew heavy in my arms,
and I made her a bow,
a small one,

not enough to spill
the tomatoes and eggs
out of the top,
before taking my leave.

Evening

Standing on Coney Island and Foster,
halfway out into traffic,
looking down the Avenue,
searching for some sign

in the on-coming pattern of lights
for the B-68, wondering
how on earth it could be so late,
imagining the bland face

of the fat dispatcher
indifferent to my fate,
here, on the corner, forgotten
and small, disrespected and screwed

again, it occurs to me that
maybe all of this
isn't an insult to me,
maybe I am an insult to all of this,

maybe this fluidity of traffic,
these glinting street lights,
this pulsing white noise
of engines and horns,

these particular people
in particular hats
accumulating at the corner
and then releasing pushing forward,

maybe the high-speed bicyclist,
the weird signage,
the mothers in long gray coats
and shopping bags

swinging from strollers
trying to get home,
maybe even these thoughts I am having,
this tense resentment

that clenches my chest,
is existence Herself,
maybe I am already riding
on the undulant surface

of her skin as she strides
down her Avenue
on her Errand,
and don't have to wait.

It's Too Hot

I retreat
to my room
and lie down
under the ceiling fan
and dream.

My children
find a laptop
and play shooting games
in the shade
until someone dies.

I walk into a room.
No one comes over
to shake my hand
or say hello.

Minutes pass.
Someone gets up
to get herself
a glass of water.

Returning to her seat,
she walks right through me.
The glass out in front
is cold,

and a little of it spills
as it passes through
my not entirely
compliant heart.

Fantasy

I send the two attorneys to the beach.
I tell them to build a castle together,
and then float up and down on the long slow waves,
and then lie side by side in the sand and drowse.

I recess the jury. Some of them run to
the jungle gym. Some of them push each other
on the swings. A few stand around in small groups
making up silly stuff no one believes.

I call in sick. I take off my black robe and wig,
and let myself stand around like that,
shivering a little in the early morning air,
for longer and longer intervals each day.

Taking off
your clothes
in a hurry,

and then putting them
back on
in a hurry.

DMV

You look at your shoe.
You look at the back of the head
in front of you in line.
You consider the blue in the window
up near the ceiling, how it's lovely out,
only a few clouds in the sky,
tiny ships lazily drifting by,
and begin to sense, amid all the hubbub
and white noise of the vast hall,
a quiet but overwhelming silence,
an all-pervasive silence,
a silence that is in and behind every incidental sound,
that quietly surrounds every conversation
through every plate glass window
at every station, that holds in place
every sticky and anxious and exasperated face,
that envelops every child bawling on the floor
or fiddling with cordon tape
or crawling under a chair,
a silence that is there before you speak,
and after you speak, and even more
deeply so in the middle of your speaking,
a silence that loves time, which is its toy,
and that could wait in line forever
and be happy. It is this silence you are beginning

to feel in between and underneath your heartbeat.
It is this silence that is making itself
known to you, letting you know how
very pleased it is with your silence,
how happy it is to be standing in line
in silent togetherness with you, demonstrating to you
how silence is assurance of presence,
and how, therefore, as long as you're willing
to be silent and patient and wait,
you will never be alone.

Wide

I was sent this ache in my jaw,
this weird throb in my tooth,
and was given the dark length of a night
with which to sit up and watch.

When I opened the icebox I received
the gift of a cold pack to strap
to the side of my face and become the very
picture of silly desolation.

Meanwhile, from behind enemy lines,
a lonely air balloon has drifted back to me.
Adorned in jaunty scarf and goggles,
Pain is riding in his basket.

He waves to me and drops a brick.
It lands at my feet with a thud
that sends another wave
through the root of my face. I bend over

and un-rubberband the message
from its weight. It says: "The more you feel,
the more intensely your self
will want to feel." I look up, but he's already

moved on, a colorful speck in the sky,
which is a rollicking and beautiful blue,
but not at all like walking out the door,
or unconditionally saying yes,

or being asked to lie back in a chair
and open your mouth wide.

Idea for a B Movie

The drone flies over
the field to measure
soil moisture, the optimal
sowing schedule.

Eliminate the farmer.
Take out the husband,
the stand-in for God,
and God. Pave him over.

Turn myth into movie.
Put Earth in chains,
and make her fornicate
with machines,

while we watch on screens,
our green thumbs twitching.

Instead

Joe Elliot

for Bob Nichols

Walking through the delicious
wet woods of early Spring,
the sound of my self carefully
stepping over the furled ferns
here and there pushing up
through the slick floor
of deciduous rot—lacquered layers
of leaves, fallen limbs in various
stages of reclamation—is drowned
out by some sudden but hidden
rhythmic engine. Apparently, there is
a temporary reconstruction project
again underway in the hollow
by the Sugar Shack, this year
a little more dilapidated,
caved in. A brown body is rising;
a murky soup of the dead
is stewing and stirring to this
terrific buzzsaw din, this dirge
of the collective, the lively individual
contributions to which are subsumed,
protected, and thus persist,
although warily, growing quieter
as we approach. We take
a few more steps and they
stop entirely, settle on the black

surface, or delve under mud
and wait. I am dismayed,
feel my own intrusion, and stop
to wait too. But Walter,
my ten year old, continues,
oblivious to the newborn
underlying silence of the woods,
persists to the foul water's
edge, his eager eyes picking out
a floating pair
of other eyes – Look!

Walter Making Water

I can see
the arc of Walter's

spray from behind
the buttonwood that grows

out of the tidal
rocks, and can hear

it satisfactorily
splatter the sea water,

but cannot see
the water or Walter.

Joe Elliot

When you go to get
a new pencil from
the place you get
new pencils from,

but have not looked
for the old one
you were using
the night before,

haven't even thought
of looking for it,
what you think
and write with that

new one will be
immeasurably less
ground down
and true.

Instead

Some people do not think
about the value of a tree,
how long it takes to grow,
how it cleans and freshens the air,
the deep shade it affords
in summer, and how it takes
the bite out of the bitter
winter winds. They are unenthusiastic
about the prospect of spending a Spring
afternoon gazing at pink blossoms,
or raking leaves and plucking fruit
in the Fall. They are unmoved
by the sounds of proximate life,
the chittering of squirrels and birds
nesting in its upper branches,
and the long term benefits this chattering
can have on the heart, and afraid
that someday a heavy rain
or wind or sudden crack of
lightning may cause the tree to fall
and cave in their bedroom roof,
or crush their minivan,
or raise their insurance premiums,
they cut it down. They do not think
to cut down the house
and take to the tree. The tree
is made of wood, too, and surely
its warm wide arms would be
willing to gather them up, as well.

Instead of adjusting the speed
of your gear to engage the gear

closest to you, which in turn engages
another gear, or even several

others neighboring it, and so on, fanning out
into a functional complexity of which

your gear may feel, in its inertial
contribution, a part, but whose infinite

and deeply dispersed intention
it can hardly glimpse,

you take a more lonely pleasure
in its disengaged perfection of shape,

its wild spinning in place,
its unencumbered teeth.

Outside the Playing Fields

In looking at the art and recreation
of the Southeastern Indians
we will often wish that we knew
more about the underlying social factors.

For example, even though we know
much about the Southeastern Indian ballgame—
how the participant stood
as he tossed out the stone roller,

the broken stick that signified the end of the game,
the pillbox hat,
the Mangum flounce,
the heart-shaped apron

that echoed the contestant's beaded forelock,—
we do not know the specific nature
of the social and political forces
which led them to play it with such ferocity.

And although, to a lesser extent, we know
the basic rules of Chunkey,—the players would roll
out a disc and then vie to see whose spear
would land closest to this target—

what we do not understand
is why the Indians would sometimes bet
the last thing they owned
on the outcome of the game,

why, having lost this bet, participants
would sometimes humiliate or mutilate themselves,
or even take their lives. In general,
we sense that the players of these games

were motivated by social factors
that lie outside the playing field,
but we cannot be specific
about what those living factors were.

After Pessoa

When the wind sighed before the dawn
what was the velocity of this wind? At what
frequency did this movement of air do its sighing?
And was this sigh verifiable as such?
For what are the signs of a sigh?
What are its symptoms? Where is the data
supporting this early morning exhalation?
And the reporter? Who is the reporter? A poet?

They are certainly not very reliable.
They stay up all night and call in sick.
They are prone to depressions and ecstasies,
so much so that they routinely botch their careers
and abandon their children. When
they're not jumping off buildings
or the backs of boats, when they're not
pulling triggers with their toes, they sit there
bloated and stupefied from the medications
they've taken to be fit to be trotted out
for a public appearance or two.

Give me an engineer any day of the week.
They are not taken to producing
emotive mutterings out of thin air.

To them the wind is just the wind.
It has a force and a direction and can be harnessed,
which is wonderful enough in and of itself
without having to be gently stroking my weary cheek.
The engineer's wind is humble enough
to push a mill that makes this light
bulb hanging from my bedroom ceiling glow
so I don't have to wait for the sun to come up,
and when the engineer dives off the stern,
he makes the littlest of splashes
because he knows the rigging and sail
he's designed will continue to pull
his lovely hull at a steady rate
farther and farther away from him.

Park Manor Home for Adults,

sandwiched between a car wash
and a restaurant supply store
on Coney Island Avenue and C,
is six long blocks from the Park.

It is not presided over by a portly lord
drinking mead by an open fire.
It is a non-descript
60's brick-face edifice

whose windows slide sideways
and out which its residents peer
after downing doses from plastic
cups in the morning.

And although this is their street address,
and although there is some familiar
camaraderie among them,
those who live here were some time ago

set free from their homes
and have been wandering ever since.
And although many are two
or three times the age

Joe Elliot

that might characterize them as such,
and unless by this term you mean someone
walking around with his fly open
or shit in his pants,

or talking to himself on the corner,
or waving his fist and cursing out
a flock of pigeons overhead,
these cannot be called adults.

Idea for a B Movie

My heart is a kite
you release and set flying
up and up
on a long string.

Tugging and tugging against this string
in the strong wind,
darting and veering
to and fro,

I appear to be dancing,
and my long excessively colored tail
that so furiously flutters
and snaps

in the strong wind to steady me,
to keep me from
the sudden
nosedive, from this distance

appears to be waving cheerfully to you,
to be trying to entertain you,
but you
have tied your end

of the string to the bench
on which you sit,
very tiny
and faraway, exchanging words

Joe Elliot

with your new friend
which I cannot hear.

Country Western Poem

The only time
I cry now

is when I'm driving my car
and it's raining out

and I turn on the radio
and I hear

one of those songs
that used to make me cry

in my cups
only I do not have

any cups
anymore.

Let Maybe Be

Maybe I'll never get to unbutton Farah Fawcett's
blouse. Maybe I'll never walk out
onto the deck of my tropical getaway.
Maybe my Power Ball number is
never going to come up. Maybe the dead
don't talk they only listen. Maybe I
never actually went to the prom. Maybe that
Volvo I owned is still broken down
on the side of the road. Maybe I'll never eat
escargot or sip Pernod in Toulouse.
Maybe I'll never get to go to heaven
or even hell. Maybe all those things I thought
about doing a long time ago it's too late
to do now. Maybe I'll be standing on line
at the DMV when my name is called
at the Hall of Vital Statistics. Maybe I'll make
an unforgivable mistake. Maybe I'll never
get around to reading all those books
on my shelves. Maybe I'll end up
in limbo forever. Maybe self-loathing
is a kind of decadence.

Grand Theft Auto Five (Walter Has A Cold)

Earlier I asked Walter to get off,
and it seems like he's off
because you can't hear the car crash,
and the trash talk,
and the guns going off.

But when I look up from my grading
he's still in front of the screen,
headphones on,
and a man is holding up a store,
and it's from his point of view.

Even from across the room,
you are the gunman
and you point it at the store owner,
and when he reaches for
something under the counter,

you shoot him once in the chest
and once in the head,
and his blood splatters on the wall
and the counter
and the register,

but the sound is off,
completely off,
so that what you hear is
the click of a mouse
and Walter breathing.

For Some Reason

I was sure
the card
on the table
said NO.

Then I thought
for some reason
it might
be saying ON.

Together of course
they say NOON,
the sun
directly overhead

looking down
for that shadow
that has withdrawn
inside you,

reluctant to spill
out either to
the left
or the right.

Two Eyes

One for me
and one for
him to look
out of.

Now I don't
look so much
out mine as
look out his

to see
what else he
might be
looking at.

Twice A Day Kitchen Clocks All Over The World Read 9:11

Does this mean that somehow embedded in the deep
infrastructure of our worldwide simultaneous
interdependence, that buried in every microchip of
every electronic device, all of which have become
extensions of our bodies, so that therefore all there is
is one body, really, one that we share, so that
therefore, by extension, blissfully asleep in every
cell of every citizen's torso and limbs and nails
is this small but living share of responsibility
digitally blinking at him or her for two one minute
intervals each day? That this slight window of
gradual daily awakening is specifically designed
to be no more and no less than he or she can learn
to admit and shoulder? And that therefore it wasn't
simply some other and some other way of life
attacking us and our way of life? That it wasn't
just black and white? So that over time, while
breakfast dishes were being gathered and scraped
and rinsed and put in dishwashers everywhere,
while ice cream was being scooped into dessert bowls
all over the world, this devastating blame must've
been spreading wordlessly and radially from
flagged locations in Afghanistan outward,
incrementally creeping from continent to continent
one day one hour one minute at a time in order to be

shared more honestly and equally? So that it really
was this one body politic cannibalizing this one
body politic? So that the un-medicated ego of
all of us, unwilling to face the dimming fantasy
of infinite growth, had no place to go, and so
turned inward into auto-assault mode, rampaging
there terribly and electronically and cellularly
and silently and blinkingly? Or was it really just
this shadowy Dick Cheney guy and his subalterns?

Politics

George?
What?
Did you brush your teeth?
No.
Go brush your teeth.
Dad?
What?
Do you know who brushed their teeth?
Who?
Hitler. Hitler brushed his teeth.
Good, George. Go brush your teeth.
Dad?
Yes?
Do you know who brushed their teeth?
Who, George?
Stalin. Stalin brushed his big white teeth.
Good, George. Go brush your teeth.
Dad?
What is it, George?
Do you know who brushed their teeth?
Who, George?
Osama Bin Laden. Osama Bin Laden brushed his teeth.
Really? He brushed his teeth?
Every day.
Good. Go brush your teeth.
Dad?
What is it now?

Do you know who never brushed their teeth?
Who?
Jesus. Jesus never ever brushed his teeth.
And what happened to him?
Dad?
What?

Tent as Poem

Dear Mayor Bloomberg,
because the erection
of a modest tent city
in a small private
downtown park
can in no way even begin
to scratch let alone dent
the steeply mirroring global guns and money
walls these flimsy temporary dwellings do protest,
and because those sleeping unplugged from
this global money and guns openly in bags
at the very bottom of this unsunny canyon
are like the sudden and scattered emergence
of mushrooms among the shadowy
roots of a climax forest's odorous floor
after a light rain the night before,
then it must be a merely symbolic act
of free speech, then these ropes and pegs and poles
and fabric fluttering in the wind
and rain are actual words
emerging from the mouths of habitats,
if not babes, and therefore must be protected
as any civic right would
by any good citizen
or mushroom-gatherer of the world.
Thank You.
Sincerely,
Mr. Elliot

ABOUT THE AUTHOR

Joe Elliot is the author of *Opposable Thumb* (subpress, 2006) and *Homework* (Lunar Chandelier, 2010). He teaches English and lives with his wife and their three sons in Brooklyn.

54506664R00100

Made in the USA
Charleston, SC
02 April 2016